DINOSAURS

Text/Consultant: Dr. Paul M. A. Willis
Illustrators: David Kirshner, James McKinnon

Published by
The National Geographic Society
John M. Fahey, Jr., President and Chief Executive Officer
Gilbert M. Grosvenor, Chairman of the Board
Nina D. Hoffman, Senior Vice President
William R. Gray, Vice President and Director, Book Division
Barbara Lalicki, Director of Children's Publishing
Barbara Brownell, Senior Editor
Mark A. Caraluzzi, Marketing Manager
Vincent P. Ryan, Manufacturing Manager

Library of Congress Catalog Number: 96-068856
ISBN: 0-7922-3444-8

Produced for the National Geographic Society by Weldon Owen Pty Ltd
43 Victoria Street, McMahons Point, NSW 2060, Australia
A member of the Weldon Owen Group of Companies
Sydney • San Francisco

Chairman: Kevin Weldon
President: John Owen
Publisher: Sheena Coupe
Managing Editor: Ariana Klepac
Text Editor: Robert Coupe
Editorial Assistant: Anne Ferrier
Art Director: Sue Burk
Designer: Mark Thacker
Production Manager: Caroline Webber

Film production by Mandarin Offset
Printed in Mexico

MY FIRST
POCKET
GUIDE

DINOSAURS

Dr. Paul M. A. Willis

**NATIONAL
GEOGRAPHIC
SOCIETY**

INTRODUCTION

Dinosaurs lived on the earth for 160 million years. That's about 320 times as long as humans have existed. Up till now, more than 780 types of dinosaur have been discovered. Everything we know about them comes from the fossils they left behind. You can learn more about fossils on page 6.

There were many different types of dinosaurs and they lived at different times. Some were as big as whales, while others were as small as crows. Some were meat eaters—fierce and dangerous hunters that preyed on other dinosaurs and animals. Some were gentle plant eaters. Some dinosaurs were fast runners, and others lumbered along slowly.

In some ways, dinosaurs were like each other. All stood on straight back legs extending down from their bodies, not sprawling out to the side like reptiles' legs. They had front legs, also called arms, that varied in length. Dinosaurs also laid eggs and had scaly skin, and they all lived on land. None lived in the seas, but a few feathered dinosaurs flew through the air. No one knows what color dinosaurs were, because fossils do not show this.

HOW TO USE THIS BOOK

In this book, you will read about dinosaurs in the order in which they lived on earth—from the earliest to the most recent. Each spread in this book tells you about one kind of dinosaur. It gives you information about its behavior, when and where it lived, what its name means, how big it was from head to tail, and what it ate. A shaded map shows you where fossils of the dinosaur have been found in the world. Discover an unusual fact about the dinosaur in the "Field Notes," and see what it looked like in its natural environment in the large picture. If you find a word you do not know, look it up in the Glossary on page 76.

WHAT IS A FOSSIL?

Fossils are the remains of animals and plants that lived long ago. Fossils usually form when an animal or plant becomes covered with sand, mud, or other material soon after it dies. Safely hidden away from other animals that might destroy the body, the dead animal slowly turns to stone.

Shell fossil

After thousands or millions of years, rain, rivers, and ice can wear away the rock from around the fossil, and scientists are able to find it. Sometimes people find fossils lying on the ground, but usually they have to dig them up from below the surface of the earth. By studying fossils, scientists can find out what life was like in the distant past.

All sorts of animals and plants can become fossils. Animals that have hard parts, such as shells or bones, are most likely to become fossils. Fossils

Fossilized *Triceratops* skeleton

Fossilized *Diplodocus* and *Apatosaurus* bones

can also be of an egg or even just a footprint. Dinosaur fossils are only very rarely found by scientists.

THE AGE OF THE DINOSAURS

The first dinosaurs appeared on earth about 230 million years ago, and the last ones died out 65 million years ago. People often call this time span "The Age of the Dinosaurs," but scientists call it the Mesozoic (MEZ-uh-ZOH-ik) era. It is divided into three periods—the Triassic (try-ASS-ic) period, the Jurassic (juh-RASS-ic) period, and the Cretaceous (cruh-TAY-shus) period. During this time, dinosaurs shared the earth with a number of other animals. These included flying reptiles with wings made of skin, and sea creatures. Sometimes these animals are mistaken for dinosaurs.

TIME LINE OF LIFE ON EARTH

MILLIONS OF YEARS AGO	ERA	PERIOD	
Present 1.64	Cenozoic	Quaternary	Humans appear
65	Cenozoic	Tertiary	Age of mammals
65	Mesozoic	Cretaceous	Dinosaurs die out
145	Mesozoic	Jurassic	Dinosaurs dominate
208	Mesozoic	Triassic	Dinosaurs appear
245	Paleozoic	Permian	Mammal-like reptiles dominate
290	Paleozoic	Carboniferous	Reptiles appear
362	Paleozoic	Devonian	Fishes dominate
408	Paleozoic	Silurian	Giant sea scorpions; first plants
439	Paleozoic	Ordovician	First animals with backbones
510	Paleozoic	Cambrian	First animals with shells
570	Proterozoic	Vendian	First soft-bodied animals
610	Proterozoic	1000	First animal traces
2500	Archaean	3500	First algae and bacteria
4000 4600	Archaean		Origin of the earth

At the beginning of the Mesozoic era, all the continents of the world were joined together to form one huge landmass, or "supercontinent," called Pangaea (pan-JEE-uh). Over many millions of years, this slowly broke up into the continents that we know today.

Flying reptile

In the early part of the Mesozoic era, everywhere was hot and dry. As time went by, the climate became more moist and humid. Toward the end of the Mesozoic era, seasons like the ones we know today began to develop.

As the Mesozoic era closed, many kinds of animals and plants disappeared, including the dinosaurs. Perhaps a large meteorite struck the earth, or erupting volcanoes wiped them out. Or perhaps they died out when the climate suddenly changed. We still do not know the reason for their disappearance.

EORAPTOR

 *Eoraptor* is the oldest known dinosaur. This little meat-eating creature stalked smaller animals as it ran through the undergrowth of fern forests. It had sharp claws for grabbing prey.

WHERE AND WHEN IT LIVED:

SOUTH AMERICA

Fossils of *Eoraptor* have been found in Argentina, in South America. It lived in the Triassic period.

DESCRIPTION:

✻ NAME
Eoraptor (EE-oh-RAP-tor) means "dawn hunter." It is the oldest dinosaur that we know of.

✻ SIZE
Eoraptor was just over three feet long.

✻ DIET
Eoraptor ate small lizards and mammal-like reptiles.

✻ MORE
Eoraptor may have scavenged food from creatures killed by large reptiles.

With its long back legs, *Eoraptor* was a swift runner.

Like all dinosaurs, *Eoraptor* had straight back legs extending down from its body. It also had scaly skin.

11

HERRERASAURUS

With its long legs for running, sharp claws for grabbing prey, and daggerlike teeth for tearing flesh, *Herrerasaurus* was a dangerous predator. Two small horns above its eyes protected it from enemies.

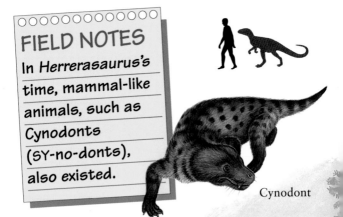

FIELD NOTES

In *Herrerasaurus*'s time, mammal-like animals, such as Cynodonts (SY-no-donts), also existed.

Cynodont

Herrerasaurus used its long tail for balance.

SOUTH AMERICA

Fossils of *Herrerasaurus* have been found in Argentina, in South America. It lived in the Triassic period.

DESCRIPTION:

✳ NAME
Herrerasaurus (hair-RAIR-uh-SORE-uhs) was named after the farmer, Victorino Herrera, who discovered it.

✳ SIZE
Herrerasaurus was ten feet long.

✳ DIET
It had sharp, curved teeth for slicing flesh. It ate reptiles.

✳ MORE
Its jaw could slide sideways to help it swallow large chunks of meat.

PLATEOSAURUS

As it browsed among ferns and pine trees, *Plateosaurus* stood on its back legs to reach high into the trees, to gather the freshest leaves. It had long claws on each hand that it used to rake plants into its mouth.

Plateosaurus's long neck helped it reach the treetops.

WHERE AND WHEN IT LIVED:

Fossils of *Plateosaurus* have been found in France, Germany, and Switzerland. It lived in the Triassic period.

DESCRIPTION:

✳ NAME
Plateosaurus (PLAT-ee-uh-SORE-uhs) means "broad lizard."

✳ SIZE
Plateosaurus was about 26 feet long— as long as a small truck.

✳ DIET
Plateosaurus was a plant eater. It had leaf-shaped teeth for cutting up leaves.

✳ MORE
It also used its long claws to defend itself against meat-eating predators.

FIELD NOTES
Although it could stand on its hind legs, Plateosaurus usually walked on all fours, with its tail off the ground.

COELOPHYSIS

 Long and slender *Coelophysis* gathered in large groups to hunt, as well as to socialize. These creatures were fast runners. Because they were lightly built, they probably did not attack large prey.

WHERE AND WHEN IT LIVED:

NORTH AMERICA

Fossils of *Coelophysis* have been found in Arizona and New Mexico. It lived in the Triassic period.

DESCRIPTION:

❋ NAME
Coelophysis (SEEL-uh-FIE-sis) means "hollow form."

❋ SIZE
Coelophysis was ten feet long.

❋ DIET
It ate small lizards, mammal-like reptiles, and baby dinosaurs. It had long jaws with sharp, saw-edged teeth.

❋ MORE
Coelophysis had hollow bones that made it light so it could run faster.

Alert and agile, *Coelophysis* had claws on its hands to grab its prey.

17

DILOPHOSAURUS

Large but lightly built, *Dilophosaurus* moved swiftly but silently through the forest in search of food. It had two bony crests on its head, which were probably brightly colored.

FIELD NOTES

Dilophosaurus's head crests may have been used to attract a mate or to scare off rivals.

Dilophosaurus often hunted for small prey, such as lizards, in the undergrowth.

Fossils of *Dilophosaurus* have been found in Arizona and in China. It lived in the Jurassic period.

DESCRIPTION:

✳ NAME
Dilophosaurus (die-LOAF-uh-SORE-uhs) means "two-crested lizard."

✳ SIZE
Dilophosaurus was almost 20 feet long.

✳ DIET
It was a meat eater. It hunted small, plant-eating dinosaurs and reptiles.

✳ MORE
It had long legs so it could run fast, and a long tail for balance. It had sharp teeth and claws for attacking its prey.

SCUTELLOSAURUS

A suit of bony armor protected *Scutellosaurus* against attacks from meat-eating dinosaurs. It had rows of bony lumps and nodules along its back, sides, and tail. The bony plates were called scutes (SKYOOTS).

Scutellosaurus's bony armor resembled a crocodile's scales.

WHERE AND WHEN IT LIVED:

NORTH AMERICA

Fossils of *Scutellosaurus* have been found in Arizona. It lived in the Jurassic period.

DESCRIPTION:

✳ NAME
Scutellosaurus (SKYOO-teh-luh-SORE-uhs) means "bony-plated lizard."

✳ SIZE
Scutellosaurus was about the size of a large dog, not including its tail.

✳ DIET
It had tiny teeth that it used to cut up plants that grew close to the ground.

✳ MORE
Scutellosaurus could run fast on its back legs, or move slowly on all four legs.

FIELD NOTES

Scutellosaurus's tail was more than two and a half times the length of its body. It was used for balance.

HETERODONTOSAURUS

Tiny *Heterodontosaurus* could run swiftly to escape its predators. But if it did have to fight, it may have slashed at its attacker with the large, stabbing teeth near the front of its mouth.

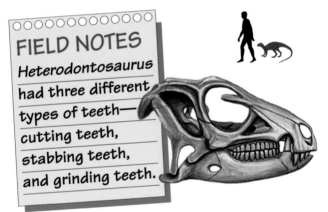

FIELD NOTES

Heterodontosaurus had three different types of teeth—cutting teeth, stabbing teeth, and grinding teeth.

Heterodontosaurus used to hide beneath plants to escape from its enemies.

WHERE AND WHEN IT LIVED:

AFRICA

Fossils of *Heterodontosaurus* have been found in southern Africa. It lived in the Jurassic period.

DESCRIPTION:

✳ NAME
The name *Heterodontosaurus* (HET-er-uh-DONT-uh-SORE-uhs) means "different-teeth lizard."

✳ SIZE
Heterodontosaurus was four feet long.

✳ DIET
It fed mainly on tough plants. It may also have eaten insects.

✳ MORE
The lower jaw had a horny beak, which was used to snip leaves off plants.

APATOSAURUS

Massive *Apatosaurus* was almost as long as a tennis court, and weighed as much as five elephants! It probably slept standing up because if it laid down, it would have had too much trouble getting up again.

Apatosaurus had a long, whiplike tail that it may have used to lash out at attackers.

WHERE AND WHEN IT LIVED:

Fossils of *Apatosaurus* have been found in North America and Mexico. It lived in the Jurassic period.

DESCRIPTION:

✳ **NAME**
Apatosaurus (uh-PAT-uh-SORE-uhs) means "deceptive lizard."

✳ **SIZE**
Apatosaurus was 69 feet long.

✳ **DIET**
It grazed on ferns and leaves from the treetops. It probably ate almost nonstop to provide energy for its huge body.

✳ **MORE**
It had a large claw on each front foot that it used like a dagger.

FIELD NOTES
Apatosaurus used its long, peglike teeth to strip leaves from branches.

DIPLODOCUS

Groups of 20 to 30 giant *Diplodocus* roamed across open plains. When family groups were moving, they kept the young animals in the middle of the pack to protect them from predators.

FIELD NOTES

The *Diplodocus* was built like a suspension bridge—its legs like the pylons, and its back like the arch.

Staying close together in groups, *Diplodocus* could graze safely.

WHERE AND WHEN IT LIVED:

NORTH AMERICA

Fossils of *Diplodocus* have been found in Colorado, Utah, and Wyoming. It lived in the Jurassic period.

DESCRIPTION:

✴ NAME
Diplodocus (di-PLOD-uh-kuhs), means "double-beam lizard." It gets its name from the shape of some of its tail bones.

✴ SIZE
Diplodocus was 89 feet long.

✴ DIET
It used its long neck to reach the tastiest leaves at the tops of trees.

✴ MORE
The large claws on each back foot helped it to grip onto muddy ground.

BRACHIOSAURUS

One of the largest dinosaurs, *Brachiosaurus* weighed as much as ten elephants. It used its heavy tail like a club to defend itself against attackers. Its front legs were longer than its hind legs.

Its neck was so long that *Brachiosaurus* could reach the treetops without rearing up on its back legs.

WHERE AND WHEN IT LIVED:

Fossils from the Jurassic and Cretaceous periods have been found in Europe, Africa, and North America.

DESCRIPTION:

✳ NAME
Its long front legs give *Brachiosaurus* (BRAK-ee-uh-SORE-uhs) its name, which means "arm lizard."

✳ SIZE
Brachiosaurus grew 82 feet long.

✳ DIET
Brachiosaurus swallowed stones to grind up food in its stomach.

✳ MORE
Brachiosaurus's nostrils were on the top of its head.

FIELD NOTES

A giraffe stands 14 feet tall. But if a giraffe stood next to a Brachiosaurus, the giraffe would look tiny!

STEGOSAURUS

 As *Stegosaurus* lumbered along on all fours, the large, bony, triangular plates along its back and the sharp spikes on the end of its tail helped protect it against predators.

WHERE AND WHEN IT LIVED:

NORTH AMERICA

Fossils of *Stegosaurus* have been found in Colorado, Utah, and Wyoming. It lived in the Jurassic period.

DESCRIPTION:

✳ **NAME**
Stegosaurus (STEG-uh-SORE-uhs) means "roofed lizard." Scientists first thought its bony plates laid flat like roof tiles.

✳ **SIZE**
Stegosaurus grew almost 30 feet long.

✳ **DIET**
It used its small, weak teeth to cut up leaves from low-growing plants.

✳ **MORE**
Stegosaurus's front legs were only half as long as its back legs.

Stegosaurus had huge spikes at the end of its tail that it used for whacking predators.

Kentrosaurus

FIELD NOTES
Other related dinosaurs had different kinds of spikes and bony plates on their bodies.

Polacanthus

CERATOSAURUS

With a short burst of speed, *Ceratosaurus* would charge out of its hiding place and pounce on its prey. Its powerful claws firmly held the victim, while its large, fanglike teeth ripped the animal to pieces.

Its huge jaws and sharp teeth made *Ceratosaurus* a skillful predator.

WHERE AND WHEN IT LIVED:

Fossils of *Ceratosaurus* have been found in North America and in Africa. It lived in the Jurassic period.

DESCRIPTION:

✳ NAME
Ceratosaurus (suh-RAT-uh-SORE-uhs) means "horned lizard."

✳ SIZE
Ceratosaurus grew to 19 feet long.

✳ DIET
It was a meat-eating dinosaur. It preyed on other dinosaurs.

✳ MORE
It had large, powerful jaws. It had a horn on its nose, a little like a rhinoceros's.

FIELD NOTES

A *Ceratosaurus* probably used its large, sharp nose horn in fights with rival *Ceratosaurus*.

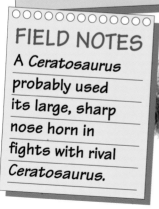

ALLOSAURUS

With many blade-like, cutting teeth, grasping hands with long, sharp claws, and long, powerful back legs, a single *Allosaurus* could chase and kill animals as big as itself, or even bigger.

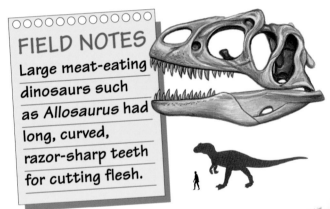

FIELD NOTES
Large meat-eating dinosaurs such as Allosaurus had long, curved, razor-sharp teeth for cutting flesh.

Allosaurus may have hunted in packs to attack and kill larger dinosaurs.

WHERE AND WHEN IT LIVED:

Fossils of *Allosaurus* have been found in Africa and North America. It lived in the Jurassic period.

DESCRIPTION:

✳ **NAME**
Allosaurus (AL-uh-SORE-uhs) means "strange lizard."

✳ **SIZE**
Allosaurus grew as long as 36 feet.

✳ **DIET**
It was a meat eater that preyed on plant-eating dinosaurs.

✳ **MORE**
Like many other meat eaters, it could slide its huge jaws sideways to swallow large chunks of meat.

DRYOSAURUS

Silently stepping through the forest, *Dryosaurus* used its large eyes to look out for its enemies—the meat-eating dinosaurs. This plant-eating dinosaur had no teeth in the front of its mouth. It bit off leaves with a kind of horny beak.

Dryosaurus ate leaves and seeds, which it picked with its fingers and popped into its mouth.

WHERE AND WHEN IT LIVED:

Fossils of *Dryosaurus* have been found in North America and East Africa. It lived in the Jurassic period.

DESCRIPTION:

✷ NAME
Dryosaurus (DRY-uh-SORE-uhs) means "tree lizard." It lived among trees.

✷ SIZE
Dryosaurus grew to 13 feet long and was about the size of a large horse.

✷ DIET
It shredded leaves and plant shoots with sharp teeth in the back of its jaw.

✷ MORE
Dryosaurus had birdlike feet with three toes. It walked on two legs.

FIELD NOTES
Long back legs and a long, stiff tail helped make *Dryosaurus* a very fast runner.

COMPSOGNATHUS

 *Compsognathus* was one of the smallest dinosaurs that we know of. With two sharp-clawed fingers on each hand and many small, sharp teeth in its long jaws, it was a skillful hunter of small animals.

WHERE AND WHEN IT LIVED:

EUROPE

Fossils of *Compsognathus* have been found in Germany and France. It lived in the Jurassic period.

DESCRIPTION:

✳ NAME
Compsognathus (KOMP-soh-NAY-thus) means "pretty jaw," because of its slim, elegant jaw.

✳ SIZE
This chicken-size dinosaur was just over two feet long.

✳ DIET
It moved swiftly through the undergrowth, hunting small lizards and mammals.

✳ MORE
Its large eyes helped it to see well.

To kill prey, such as a small lizard,
Compsognathus would beat it against a rock.

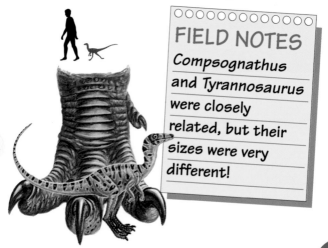

ARCHAEOPTERYX

 Try to imagine an animal that is half dinosaur and half bird. That's what *Archaeopteryx* was like. It had wings and feathers like a bird and it could fly, but the rest of its body looked like a dinosaur's.

FIELD NOTES

Like dinosaurs, *Archaeopteryx* had teeth, fingers with claws, and a long, bony tail.

Fossils of *Archaeopteryx* have been found in southern Germany. It lived in the Jurassic period.

DESCRIPTION

✳ NAME
Archaeopteryx (AR-key-OP-ter-ix) means "ancient wing."

✳ SIZE
Archaeopteryx was two feet long—about as big as a large crow.

✳ DIET
It had many small teeth, which it used to crunch up insects.

✳ MORE
Archaeopteryx might have used its long claws to help it climb trees.

Archaeopteryx may have launched itself into the air from high in a tree.

IGUANODON

 *Iguanodon* was a harmless plant eater, but it had stabbing spikes on its thumbs that could seriously injure an attacker. It moved quickly on its back legs, or walked slowly on all fours.

WHERE AND WHEN IT LIVED:

Fossils have been found in North America, Europe, and Asia. *Iguanodon* lived in the Cretaceous period.

DESCRIPTION:

＊NAME
Iguanodon (i-GWAN-uh-DON) means "iguana tooth," because its teeth look like a modern iguana lizard's teeth.

＊SIZE
Iguanodon grew almost 30 feet long.

＊DIET
It cut off leaves with its horny beak and ground them with its back teeth.

＊MORE
Bony rods along its backbone kept *Iguanodon's* back and tail stiff.

Iguanodon broke off branches with its powerful arms, then ate the leaves.

hoof

HYPSILOPHODON

Warm, moist, riverside thickets of ferns were home to the small dinosaur *Hypsilophodon*. This plant eater may have lived in small groups. Ferns and other plants kept it hidden from its enemies.

Hypsilophodon was one of the fastest dinosaurs. It ran and walked on its hind legs.

WHERE AND WHEN IT LIVED:

Fossils of *Hypsilophodon* have been found in North America and Europe. It lived in the Cretaceous period.

DESCRIPTION:

✷ NAME
Hypsilophodon (HIP-suh-LOF-uh-don) means "high-crested tooth."

✷ SIZE
Hypsilophodon was just over seven feet.

✷ DIET
Hypsilophodon had cheek pouches for storing plants in its mouth while it chewed them. It had high-crested teeth.

✷ MORE
Hypsilophodon had a long tail to help it keep its balance when running.

FIELD NOTES

Hypsilophodon had large eyes and good eyesight. This helped it to see and escape its enemies.

45

PSITTACOSAURUS

 Walking on two legs through ferns and flowering plants, *Psittacosaurus* broke branches off trees with its sharp beak, and then held them with its short, stubby fingers while it ate.

WHERE AND WHEN IT LIVED:

ASIA

Fossils of *Psittacosaurus* have been found in Asia. It lived in the Cretaceous period.

DESCRIPTION:

✷ NAME
Psittacosaurus (si-TAK-oh-SAW-rus) means "parrot lizard."

✷ SIZE
Psittacosaurus grew about as big as a medium-size dog.

✷ DIET
It had tough teeth that allowed it to eat the hard parts of plants.

✷ MORE
It swallowed stones to grind up food in its stomach.

Although it usually walked on two legs, *Psittacosaurus* went down on all fours to eat or drink.

FIELD NOTES

Psittacosaurus's parrotlike beak could snip off flowers and plants like a pair of garden shears.

DEINONYCHUS

Even though *Deinonychus* weighed no more than an adult human, it must have been a feared predator. On both of its feet was a large, hooked claw that it used to slash the bodies of its prey.

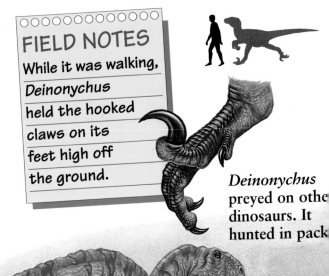

Deinonychus preyed on other dinosaurs. It hunted in pack

WHERE AND WHEN IT LIVED:

Fossils of *Deinonychus* have been found in Montana and Wyoming. It lived in the Cretaceous period.

DESCRIPTION:

✳ NAME
Deinonychus (die-NON-i-kuhs) means "terrible claw."

✳ SIZE
Deinonychus grew about ten feet long.

✳ DIET
Because it hunted in packs, *Deinonychus* could attack and kill dinosaurs much larger than itself.

✳ MORE
It had powerful back legs to help it run fast. It had strong jaws with large fangs.

SEGNOSAURUS

 *Segnosaurus* had large, powerful claws on its hands and feet, which it may have used to dig the soil as it searched for food. It probably also used them to hold its prey and to fight enemies.

WHERE AND WHEN IT LIVED:

Fossils of *Segnosaurus* have been found in Mongolia, in Asia. It lived in the Cretaceous period.

DESCRIPTION:

✳ NAME
Segnosaurus (SEG-noe-SORE-uhs) means "slow lizard."

✳ SIZE
Segnosaurus was as big as a small bus.

✳ DIET
Segnosaurus had a toothless beak and leaf-shaped teeth for eating a variety of creatures.

✳ MORE
Segnosaurus had long, muscular arms. It probably walked on its back legs.

Segnosaurus used its strong claws to rip open logs in search of food.

51

MAIASAURA

A *Maiasaura* female laid up to 20 eggs in a nest made of mud and leaves. She then covered the eggs with sand until they hatched. The newly hatched babies had weak legs and could not leave the nest for many weeks.

Large numbers of *Maiasaura* made their nests next to each other in the same area.

WHERE AND WHEN IT LIVED:

Fossils of *Maiasaura* have been found in Montana. It lived during the Cretaceous period.

DESCRIPTION:

✳ NAME
Maiasaura (MY-uh-SORE-uh) means "good mother lizard."

✳ SIZE
Maiasaura grew to almost 30 feet long.

✳ DIET
These duck-billed dinosaurs roamed in huge herds, searching for plants.

✳ MORE
They ran and walked on their long back legs, but stood on all fours when feeding or drinking near the ground.

FIELD NOTES

Both *Maiasaura* parents searched for plants for food for their young, and protected them from predators.

EDMONTONIA

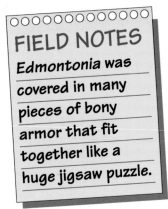

As it plodded through forests, *Edmontonia* did not need to run from attackers. Rows of bony lumps and plates on its back and tail and sharp spikes on it sides and shoulders protected it from predators.

FIELD NOTES

Edmontonia was covered in many pieces of bony armor that fit together like a huge jigsaw puzzle.

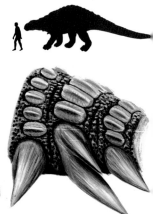

Edmontonia had shoulder spikes that it thrust at an attacking predator.

WHERE AND WHEN IT LIVED:

Fossils of *Edmontonia* have been found in North America. It lived in the Cretaceous period.

DESCRIPTION:

✳ NAME
Edmontonia (ED-muhn-TONE-ee-uh) was named after Edmonton, in Alberta, Canada, where it was first found.

✳ SIZE
Edmontonia grew to 23 feet long.

✳ DIET
It had small teeth with ridged surfaces which it used to cut up leaves and shoots.

✳ MORE
It had large pouches in its cheeks where it could store food while it chewed.

EUOPLOCEPHALUS

Like an armored tank roaming the plains, *Euoplocephalus* was covered in a bony suit of armor with a bone-crunching club on the end of its tail. It had bony spikes over its shoulders, and even had armor in its eyelids.

Faced with danger, a *Euoplocephalus* would swing its mighty tail club.

WHERE AND WHEN IT LIVED:

NORTH AMERICA

Fossils of *Euoplocephalus* have been found in North America. It lived in the Cretaceous period.

DESCRIPTION:

✳ NAME
Euoplocephalus (YOO-ope-low-SEF-uh-luhs) means "well-armored head."

✳ SIZE
Euoplocephalus grew to 23 feet long.

✳ DIET
It ate plants, which it chewed with its small, ridged teeth.

✳ MORE
Its belly was only lightly armored, but it was safe from attackers. They couldn't push over its wide, short-legged body.

FIELD NOTES

At the end of its tail was a solid, bony club that could break the ankles of an attacker.

VELOCIRAPTOR

Fast-moving *Velociraptor* was only about as big as a present-day goat. But with a huge curved claw on both its feet, it could easily kill animals twice its size. It walked and ran on two legs.

FIELD NOTES

Velociraptor's speed —and its sharp teeth and claws— would have made it a feared predator.

Swift and dangerous, a pack of *Velociraptor* easily overtook prey, such as this plant-eating dinosaur.

WHERE AND WHEN IT LIVED:

Fossils of *Velociraptor* have been found in Mongolia, in Asia. It lived in the Cretaceous period.

DESCRIPTION:

✴ NAME
Velociraptor (vuh-LOSS-uh-RAP-tor) means "speedy hunter."

✴ SIZE
Velociraptor grew six feet long, but half of this length was its stiff, rodlike tail.

✴ DIET
It preyed on plant-eating dinosaurs and may have hunted in packs.

✴ MORE
Its long, flat snout had many saw-edged teeth that cut through prey like scissors.

PROTOCERATOPS

Protoceratops lived in deserts, near sand dunes, where it made its shallow nest and laid its long, oval eggs. During the rainy season, lakes and rivers filled with water, and plants grew for *Protoceratops* to eat.

Protoceratops had to guard its eggs against egg-stealing predators.

WHERE AND WHEN IT LIVED:

Fossils of *Protoceratops* have been found in parts of Asia. It lived in the Cretaceous period.

DESCRIPTION:

✳ NAME
Protoceratops (PROE-toe-SAIR-ah-tops) means "first horn face."

✳ SIZE
Protoceratops grew less than six feet long.

✳ DIET
It snipped off plants close to the ground with its beak, then ground them down with the teeth at the back of its mouth.

✳ MORE
A broad, bony frill across the back of its neck helped protect it against predators.

FIELD NOTES
As *Protoceratops* grew older, its neck frill grew bigger, and a small, bumplike horn grew on its nose.

61

OVIRAPTOR

 With long-fingered hands tipped with sharp claws, and a sharp and dangerous horny beak, *Oviraptor* was a fierce hunter. It could even attack and kill the dangerous *Velociraptor*.

WHERE AND WHEN IT LIVED:

ASIA

Fossils of *Oviraptor* have been found in Mongolia, in Asia. It lived in the Cretaceous period.

DESCRIPTION:

＊NAME
Oviraptor (OH-vee-RAP-tor) means "egg thief."

＊SIZE
Oviraptor grew a little over six feet long.

＊DIET
Scientists once thought that it ate only eggs. They now know that it also ate small dinosaurs.

＊MORE
It had a crest on its head, and a toothless snout with a horny beak.

Oviraptor's head crest may have been used for head-butting when fighting.

○○○○○○○○○○○○○○
FIELD NOTES
Oviraptor females sat on their eggs in the nest, to keep them warm, until they hatched.

ORNITHOMIMUS

The slender, ballerina-like *Ornithomimus* belonged to a group of fast-moving dinosaurs that some people call "ostrich dinosaurs." They ran on their hind legs and could move 30 miles an hour, twice as fast as an Olympic sprinter.

Always on the move, *Ornithomimus* might fight over prey while speeding across an open plain.

WHERE AND WHEN IT LIVED:

Fossils of *Ornithomimus* have been found in North America. It lived in the Cretaceous period.

DESCRIPTION:

✳ NAME
Ornithomimus (OR-nuh-thoe-MIME-uhs) means "bird mimic."

✳ SIZE
Ornithomimus grew to just over 13 feet.

✳ DIET
It had no teeth. It probably ate small mammals and eggs, which it crushed with its beaklike snout.

✳ MORE
With its large eyes, it could see in all directions for danger.

FIELD NOTES

With long legs and long neck, *Ornithomimus* looked similar to an ostrich. But it had no feathers.

TYRANNOSAURUS

 With its powerful, four-foot-long jaw filled with deadly, seven-inch-long stabbing teeth, the massive, meat-eating *Tyrannosaurus* could kill all but the most heavily armored of dinosaurs.

WHERE AND WHEN IT LIVED:

NORTH AMERICA

Fossils of *Tyrannosaurus* have been found in North America. It lived in the Cretaceous period.

DESCRIPTION:

✳ NAME
Tyrannosaurus (tie-RAN-uh-SORE-uhs) means "tyrant lizard."

✳ SIZE
Tyrannosaurus grew more than 40 feet long—about as long as a truck.

✳ DIET
It probably hid among trees and bushes, waiting to pounce on its prey.

✳ MORE
Tyrannosaurus had tiny arms, but they could lift the weight of two adult humans.

Tyrannosaurus had powerful back legs, but it was probably too big to run very fast.

FIELD NOTES
Tyrannosaurus may have used its arms to lift itself up off the ground after lying down.

EDMONTOSAURUS

Herds of large, duck-billed *Edmontosaurus* wandered across open plains in search of plants. Their best defense against predators, such as *Tyrannosaurus*, was to stay in huge groups of thousands of animals.

FIELD NOTES

Hundreds of teeth at the back of Edmontosaurus's mouth worked like a cheese grater, grinding up plants.

If *Edmontosaurus* sensed danger, it honked to warn the rest of its group.

WHERE AND WHEN IT LIVED:

NORTH
AMERICA

Fossils of *Edmontosaurus* have been found in North America. It lived in the Cretaceous period.

DESCRIPTION:

✳ NAME
Edmontosaurus (ed-MON-tuh-SORE-uhs) was named after Edmonton, in Canada, where it was first found.

✳ SIZE
Edmontosaurus grew 43 feet long.

✳ DIET
It nipped off juicy leaves and fruits with its toothless beak.

✳ MORE
It probably walked on all fours, but ran on its hind legs when fleeing predators.

PARASAUROLOPHUS

 Trumpeting loudly across long distances through their hollow head crests, large, duck-billed *Parasaurolophus* could warn each other that danger was nearby—or they could call to mates or scare off rivals.

WHERE AND WHEN IT LIVED:

NORTH AMERICA

Fossils of *Parasaurolophus* have been found in North America. It lived in the Cretaceous period.

DESCRIPTION:

✱ NAME
The name *Parasaurolophus* (pare-uh-SORE-O-LOAF-uhs) means "like *Saurolophus*"—a related dinosaur.

✱ SIZE
Parasaurolophus grew to 33 feet long.

✱ DIET
Cheek pouches held plants in its mouth while hundreds of small teeth ground them to a pulp.

✱ MORE
It walked on two legs or on all fours.

Herds of *Parasaurolophus* could quickly clear plantlife from the treetops.

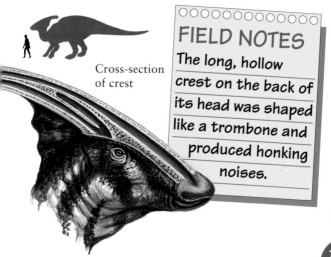

Cross-section of crest

PACHYCEPHALOSAURUS

Pachycephalosaurus had a thick round skull like a crash helmet, which protected its brain when it fought for mates or territory with other *Pachycephalosaurus*. The skull had knobs and spikes at the rim.

FIELD NOTES

When fighting, *Pachycephalosaurus* used its bony skull like a battering ram to butt heads with its rival.

Two male *Pachycephalosaurus* would fight over which one would dominate the group.

WHERE AND WHEN IT LIVED:

Fossils of *Pachycephalosaurus* have been found in North America. It lived in the Cretaceous period.

DESCRIPTION:

✳ NAME
The name *Pachycephalosaurus* (PAK-ee-SEF-uh-luh-SORE-uhs) means "thick-headed lizard."

✳ SIZE
Pachycephalosaurus grew 15 feet long.

✳ DIET
Its small, ridged teeth could only chew soft leaves, fruits, and perhaps insects.

✳ MORE
It walked on its long back legs. It used its small arms to reach branches of trees.

TRICERATOPS

Built like a huge rhinoceros and moving in large herds, *Triceratops* must have been a dangerous opponent for a meat-eating dinosaur. Three large horns and a strong, bony neck frill helped protect this giant from its enemies.

At sunset, one of the large *Triceratops* would call to the rest of the group.

WHERE AND WHEN IT LIVED:

Fossils of *Triceratops* have been found in North America. It lived in the Cretaceous period.

DESCRIPTION:

* NAME
Triceratops (try-SAIR-uh-tops) means "three-horned face."

* SIZE
Triceratops was 30 feet long—almost twice as big as a rhinoceros.

* DIET
It fed on most kinds of plants, which it cut up with its self-sharpening teeth.

* MORE
It walked on all fours. Its toes had broad hooves that protected its feet.

FIELD NOTES

Close relatives of *Triceratops* had different arrangements of horns and neck frills.

GLOSSARY

Browse To search for plants at or near head height.

Cheek pouch A pocket of skin inside the mouth of some animals, for storing food.

Climate The usual weather in a place.

Crest A ridge that sticks out of a skull or a tooth.

Flesh The soft parts of the body, between the skin and the bones.

Graze To search for plant food at or near ground level.

High-crested tooth Teeth with large crests.

Iguana A type of modern lizard.

Mammal A warm-blooded animal, usually with hair or fur, that feeds its young on milk from the mother's body.

Mate When adult males and females come together to produce young.

Meteorite A piece of rock from space that crashes to earth.

Nodule A small, hard lump.

Plains Flat, open areas of land.

Plates Thin, flat pieces of bone.

Predator Any animal that hunts other animals for food.

Prey An animal that is hunted by other animals for food.

Reptile A cold-blooded animal with scaly or leathery skin that usually lays eggs, such as a snake or lizard.

Scavenge To eat animals that are already dead, probably killed by other animals.

Socialize To live and be friendly in a group of other animals of the same kind.

Stalk To follow slowly and quietly in order to catch and kill.

Territory The place where an animal or group of animals lives. Animals defend their territory from other animals of the same type.

Thicket A place where bushes and small trees grow very closely together.

Undergrowth The lowest level of plants in a woodland or forest.

INDEX OF
DINOSAURS

ABOUT THE CONSULTANT

Dr. Paul M. A. Willis has had a lifelong interest in fossils and extinct animals, finding his first fossil when he was six years old. He studied zoology and geology at the University of Sydney and in 1995 he received his doctorate in vertebrate palaeontology for studies on Australian fossil crocodilians from the University of New South Wales. British-born and educated in Australia, he has traveled extensively throughout the world in the course of his studies. Presently based in Sydney, Australia, Paul Willis works freelance specializing in communicating earth sciences to the public, particularly children.

PHOTOGRAPHIC CREDITS

6 (top) Geolinea 6–7 (bottom) Royal Tyrrell Museum/Alberta Community Development 7 (top) Auscape/Francois Gohier 8 The Natural History Museum, London.